AF211877

JAYSON NILS

FINISH WHAT YOU START

The Ultimate Guide on How to Keep Yourself Motivated to Achieve Your Goals, Learn the Effective Ways to Motivate Yourself to Achieve Anything!

Descrierea CIP a Bibliotecii Naționale a României
JAYSON NILS
   FINISH WHAT YOU START. The Ultimate Guide To
Blogging for Beginners, Learn the Secrets and Strategies on
How You Can Build and Launch Profitable Autopilot Blogs /
Jayson Nils – Bucharest: Editura My Ebook, 2021
   ISBN

JAYSON NILS

FINISH WHAT YOU START

The Ultimate Guide on How to Keep Yourself Motivated to Achieve Your Goals, Learn the Effective Ways to Motivate Yourself to Achieve Anything!

My Ebook Publishing House
Bucharest, 2021

CONTENTS

INTRODUCTION

Learning how to motivate yourself at-will is one of the most important skills you can learn.

It doesn't matter if you're a student, entrepreneur, recent divorcee, or anything else.

Being able to keep pushing forward, and doing what you need to do, is a skill that EVERYONE should master.

This isn't just about willpower- although that's part of it.

It isn't just about your "Why", although it plays a role.

Motivation isn't always about taking massive action- but it can certainly help.

Here's what Wikipedia has to say about motivation:

*"**Motivation** is a psychological feature that arouses an organism to act towards a desired goal and elicits, controls, and sustains certain goal-directed behaviors. It can be considered a driving force; a psychological one that compels or reinforces an*

action toward a desired goal. For example, hunger is a motivation that elicits a desire to eat. Motivation is the purpose or psychological cause of an action

Motivation has been shown to have roots in physiological, behavioral, cognitive, and social areas. Motivation may be rooted in a basic impulse to optimize wellbeing, minimize physical pain and maximize pleasure. It can also originate from specific physical needs such as eating, sleeping or resting, and sex.

Motivation is an inner drive to behave or act in a certain manner. "It's the difference between waking up before dawn to pound the pavement and lazing around the house all day. These inner conditions such as wishes, desires, goals, activate to move in a particular direction in behavior."

That's a pretty good explanation, but let's keep it a lot shorter.

Motivation is finding the energy and enthusiasm to accomplish your goals.

That's it.

Again- there are many other things that play a role in this.

- Your willpower
- Your environment

- Your history

- Your current situation

- Who you hang out with

- Whether you like what you're doing

- Etc.

But at the end of the day, being motivated means taking action towards what you're supposed to do.

Is it easy? No way! If it was, procrastination wouldn't be such a prevalent force in today's society.

But what I've learned over the years is that typically, the hard things are what make the biggest difference.

The hard talk with a friend.

The hard workout.

The long nights working on your business.

And once you master the ability to motivate yourself, you'll be able to do all of these things- and more- without a sweat!

So how do we do this? How do we learn how to motivate ourselves to do what needs to be done?

There are basically 3 main steps:

1) Write Your Goals

2) Identify and Focus on Your Outcomes

3) Get Social!

Too simple? Maybe- but again, it doesn't mean it's easy.

Let me show you what I mean, starting with Step 1.

Write Down Your Goals

Just about every business or mindset book I've ever read has talked about setting goals.

But there's a reason for that, right?

It's because goal-setting is a skill that is a major factor in helping people stay focused and motivated.

Plus, if so many successful people are telling you to set goals- and your brain or your not-so-successful friends are telling you goals are dumb...

Are you really listening to the right person?

If Warren Buffett, the world's greatest stock investor, told you to invest in Stock X- would you *really* invest in Stock Y instead, just because your friend told you to?

Probably not.

So why do you do that with setting goals? Brushing them off, thinking that it's just a bunch of new-age mumbo jumbo?

The bottom line is- **goals work if done correctly.**

How do you "do" goals correctly? There are a few main factors.

1) You MUST Set S.M.A.R.T. Goals

You've probably heard this before, but I'll say it again. S.M.A.R.T. stands for

- Specific
- Measurable
- Attainable
- Realistic
- Timely

The reason for doing this is that there's no ambiguity here. You either reach your goal, or you don't.

Let's take a look at 2 goals.

Goal #1: "Lose weight."

Goal #2: "I will lose 2 pounds this week by eating 1,200 calories a day, getting 7 hours of sleep every night and walking 30 minutes a day."

HUGE difference between those goals, right?

The first one isn't specific at all, it's hardly measurable, it's definitely attainable and realistic, but it's not very timely.

The second goal on the other hand, meets all 5 factors of a S.M.A.R.T. goal.

And it's easy to see if you reached your goal or not, right? At the end of this week, just weigh yourself and see if you lost the 2 pounds.

But most people don't set goals like that. Instead, it's stuff like "lose weight", or "get a promotion", or "spend more time with the kids".

Those are too ambiguous, and you're almost guaranteed not to achieve what you *really* want to.

But there's more to it when it comes to using goals to keep you motivated.

2) Review Your Goals Daily

I can't tell you how many times I've set goals... and then just COMPLETELY forgot about them.

Even if they were S.M.A.R.T. goals, it doesn't matter. Since I wasn't reviewing them on a regular basis, they were pretty much worthless to me.

The way one speaker put it- reviewing goals once a year means that they aren't really goals.

They're wishes.

A wish is something that you hope happens, but you don't really make any effort towards it.

Meanwhile, a goal is something you want to happen and work towards to *make* it happen.

Constantly.

Daily.

But it's difficult to do that if you don't keep your goals in front of you all the time.

That's why the most successful people I know review their goals at least 1-2 times a day.

In the morning, going through your goals helps remind you *why* you're gearing up for the day.

In the evening, reviewing your goals can help you look back on the day, decide the type of progress you made, and from there plan out the next day.

You can also consider reviewing your goals at lunchtime, to give you a mental "reset" so that for the afternoon, you're focused on what you need to do.

Personally, I've found that my goals are literally useless if I don't review them daily.

I'm guessing you're the same way.

So what is it gonna be?

Are you going to pursue goals? Or just make a wish list?

If you decide to set goals, great- but there's still one more point I want to make.

3) NEVER Reduce Your Goals

Did you ever have a project in school where the teacher pushed back the due date?

Or been on a program in business, and when the project goes over-budget, the boss just raises the allocated budget immediately?

These scenarios- just like lowering your goals- **should never happen.**

If you say that your goal is to lose 10 mounds this month- and halfway through you've only lost 2 pounds...

Is lowering your goal to 5 pounds the right answer?

Or is the right answer to increase your efforts?

From personal experience- as well as that from my mentors- I can tell you that lowering your goal is ALWAYS the wrong solution.

If your weight loss is going to slow, you've got to pick up the pace. Eat more salads, walk more, stop eating sugar- whatever it takes.

If your sales projections aren't doing well, figure out a way to boost them. Don't lower your expectations!

This goes for any goal, period.

Don't change the goal just because things aren't going like you expected.

Instead, adapt, stay focused on the prize, and charge even harder towards it.

Because once you lower your goals one time, it just gets easier to do it again. And again.

Before you know it- your goals don't really mean anything. They aren't goals anymore. Not really.

They're more like wishes that you review on a regular basis.

To give another example-

If I just got laid off, and my goal was to make $1,000 by the end of the month so that I can pay the rent.

And by the 25th, I've only made $100.

Is the right answer to lower my goal to $500?

Of course not- because that wouldn't even let me pay the rent!

So what happens then? I don't want to go get thrown out on the streets.

On the flip side- if I keep the same goal- and just work harder to achieve it- I get to stay in my house!

This is why the second part of the equation- Identify Your Outcomes- plays such a crucial role.

But that's for the next chapter.

Identify Your Outcomes

Short-term motivation relies on looking at the big picture.

Even though something like a short motivational video or quote can help get you pumped- you still need to know what you're getting pumped for, right?

In that last section, I was talking about trying to make $1,000 by the end of the month.

To keep it simple, we'll say that you have 2 main outcomes for this scenario:

Outcome #1: I achieve my goal, pay the rent, and get another month to find a job, build up a side business, or whatever else is needed to pay the rent.

Outcome #2: I don't achieve my goal and get kicked out onto the streets with all of my stuff.

Now- that's a very simplistic way of looking at it, but it proves my point.

To *really* stay motivated, you've got to look at what happens due to your actions.

Will eating that fast food every day help you get lean and mean, or make you gain weight?

Can arguing with your spouse about the little things all the time really strengthen your marriage, or is it making everything worse?

Will watching TV or playing video games instead of working on your business really help you achieve your goals?

You have a reason- a "Why" for the goals that you set.

That "Why" is probably the positive outcomes that can come from achieving the goals you set.

Maybe it's letting you spend more time with your kids.

It could be to be healthier, have less pain and live longer to spend time with family or travel.

Maybe it's so you have financial freedom to sit at home all day and watch soap operas.

I dunno.

But whatever it is, that's only HALF of the equation.

What Happens if You DON'T Reach Your Goals?

Most people only talk about the good outcomes that can happen when you reach your goals.

You can buy X, or pay off Y loan, or you can work for yourself, or whatever.

But there's the other side of the coin.

If you don't put in the time and effort to reach the goals you set- what happens?

- You might lose your job
- You can lose the house
- Your spouse can leave you
- You could get terminally ill
- Your kids won't like you
- Your friends might stop calling

Whatever the possible outcomes are- you have to identify them.

Both the positive AND negative sides.

Now- I'm not telling you to throw in EVERY single possible outcome.

Because you never *really* know what's going to happen, despite what some people say about controlling their lives.

But at the same time- you can give a really good guess, right?

If your goal is to lose 10 pounds and you only lose 5- well, that means you'll still feel bad for yourself, have poor self-esteem and confidence, and more.

But if you do lose the full 10 pounds, you'll feel better about yourself, look better, possibly attract more of the opposite gender, have better confidence, and more.

Do you see my point here?

You see, motivation isn't JUST about the warm-and-fuzzy feelings that most people tend to associate it with.

You've probably heard that you can motivate people with carrots (time off work, bonuses, food, etc.) versus sticks (getting fired, going to timeout, etc.)

This is the exact same thing.

The only difference is **you're motivating yourself.**

But the cool thing is that you don't have to choose one or the other to focus on.

In fact, I recommend that you keep both in mind. That way you can be motivated by both the carrot AND the stick.

How do you do this? Simple.

For each goal, make a table underneath it. This table lists the positive outcomes on the left side, and negative on the right.

So it might look like this:

Goal: I will lose 10 pounds this month by eating 1,200 calories a day, getting 7 hours of sleep every night and walking 30 minutes a day."

Positive Outcomes	Negative Outcomes
I'll have more confidence and selfesteem	I'll feel like I failed
I'll take pressure off my aching knees	My knees will continue to get worse and more painful
I'll probably live longer	I'll probably die earlier
I'll have a lot more energy	I'll keep feeling too sluggish to do anything

That's all you really have to do.

That way, when you review your goals, you can also review the outcomes which came from *why* you want to achieve those goals.

Got it?

Now let's talk about the last important element- being social!

Get Social

Human beings, as much as we may act like it sometimes, are NOT good at doing things on our own.

Sure, there are plenty of things we can do as individuals.

But as a whole? We're 10x more effective working together as a group than individually.

Just a quick example, think of your breakfast.

Let's say it's usually pretty simple- a bowl of cereal with milk and an orange with some multivitamins.

Think of EVERYTHING that food went through just to get to you.

- The cereal was probably corn or wheat grown by a farmer

- Corn/wheat gets ground up and shipped to the cereal factory

- By combining the wheat with lots of other stuff, and some processing, you get the cereal

- Now it gets shipped to a distribution center, then to a grocery store

- You drive to the store in a car *you* didn't make, and buy the cereal with paper money or a credit card (again, which you didn't physically create)

- You drive back home using gas that was refined by a company

- You pour the cereal and milk (from a different farm) into a bowl (made in China) and eat it with a spoon (made on the other side of the country)

And that's JUST your cereal.

Never mind the dozens of other things you eat or use on a daily basis.

Humans work much better when we do it as a team.

Working together, we can share knowledge, tips & tricks, and experience in limitless areas- health, wealth, engineering, law- EVERYTHING.

This works for achieving your goals too.

If you keep your goals private, and never let anyone know about them...

Nobody can help you.

Nobody can motivate you.

Nobody can celebrate your victories with you.

But if you share them with your family, friends, coworkers or a mastermind group.

It's an entirely different ballgame.

When you're feeling tired and don't want to run anymore-your running buddy will help motivate you to keep going.

When it seems like your marriage just can't get any worse-that neighbor who's been married for 50 years can help put you on the right track.

When your sales numbers are struggling, having that A-type personality buddy who can sell ice to an Eskimo can motivate you and help you out.

STOP trying to do everything on your own.

It doesn't work.

Build a team, and let them help you accomplish your goals.

They'll motivate you when you're tired and struggling.

They'll give you the knowledge you need to overcome tough obstacles.

They might even make sacrifices to help you, such as lending you their workout equipment, books or editing your reports and presentations.

Why Do People Like Facebook and YouTube?

Think about it- why do people LOVE these sites?

Facebook is great for a few reasons, but one of the big ones is the "Like" feature.

When you put up some kind of comment or picture, and people "Like" it, doesn't that make you feel good?

It motivates you.

The same goes for YouTube. When some people start "follow-me" type channels for weight loss, business etc., the people who subscribe and pay attention help motivate that person.

Multiple ways!

When people are watching, you try harder.

Period.

When I was a kid, I always tried harder at karate or basketball when my parents were there.

As a teenager and college kid, my sports were always turned up a notch if girls were watching.

When you're at work, you probably try harder when your coworkers or boss is asking you for something, or watching you, right?

Of course you do.

But more than that.

People keep you accountable

They don't just motivate you, or help you when you're struggling.

They also make sure you're making forward progress towards your goals.

People who truly care for you will push and challenge you.

When you stop showing up for workouts, they'll ask.

When you start coming in to work late- they'll get on you about it.

When you revert back to treating your family poorly- an accountability partner will call you out.

That's why you need to be social.

But even more than that- **you need an accountability partner.**

When done right, accountability partners are just fantastic. They're better than just making your goals public because they will specifically seek you out to make sure you're chasing your goals.

Most people will look at you chase your goals and just cheer you on. Some might call you out if you stop trying as hard, but most won't.

Trust me.

They have enough other stuff to worry about.

Plus most people don't want to "stir the pot." They're afraid that if they call you out, you won't be friends with them anymore.

On the other hand- an accountability partner knows that's their job.

So what's the best way to use an accountability partner? Here are a few things to keep in mind:

Don't Let Family be Accountability Partners

If it's a distant cousin or something, that might be okay.

But spouses, kids, parents and siblings are off limits.

Why? Because you're going to get REALLY frustrated with your accountability partner at times.

That is, if they're good.

Why?

Because when you stop trying as hard, they'll tell you.

When you aren't doing what you're supposed to, your accountability will nag you about it. Constantly.

That's their job, right? They keep bugging you and giving you a hard time because you asked them to.

But if it's a family member doing this- you can take it personally.

You might get mad at the person, not what they're saying to you.

Instead, it's better to have a friend, neighbor or coworker who you aren't extremely close to do this.

Sure, you might get frustrated with them.

But at least you aren't getting very frustrated with your best friend, or spouse for nagging you all the time.

Make it Daily

Another thing to keep in mind is to talk to your accountability partner daily.

I've tried other timeframes, like once a week or every other day. They didn't work very well for me or the other person.

The main reason is that it just isn't enough. You need to work on your goals daily, right? Not just when you feel like it.

If you talk to your partner every single day, they make sure that happens.

Because think about what happens if you only talk once a week, say on Fridays.

The first Friday you talk, everything is great- you're moving right along.

But that weekend you slack off a bit, and by Monday or Tuesday it's hard to get back into the swing of things.

By the time next Friday rolls around, you're not working on your goals at all. And since your accountability partner didn't know, it will now be difficult for them to motivate you.

Instead, talk to them daily. This lets them motivate you on a daily basis, and help pick you up when you fall down.

Share Your Goals and Outcomes

Don't just tell your accountability partner what your goal is. That's a great start, but it's not quite enough.

You also need to tell them your *Why*.

What are the possible outcomes that can happen from this goal?

If you reach it, how much better would your life be?

Or if you don't reach it, in what ways does it negatively affect your life?

Tell them these things, so they have a clearer understanding of the big picture.

If they don't understand these, it will be harder for them to motivate you when times are tough and you're tired. They can't really speak to your heart, because they wouldn't know what it is.

This also gives them a higher ability to celebrate with you. When you lose that weight, they'll better understand how great you feel, and the accomplishment that you'd made.

Do you see now why letting other people see you goals can help you?

You aren't an island! You have a lot of people around you that can help; you just have to let them.

From the Trenches

I was originally going to stop at the last chapter- but I felt the need to throw in one more.

These are a few things I've learned over the years about myself regarding motivation. Take it or leave it, but this is what works for me!

Work Fast

One thing I've learned about myself is that my best way to get something done is quickly.

What I mean is that if I'm motivated and inspired to do something, I've got to do it *now.*

Not tomorrow.

Not later this afternoon.

RIGHT NOW.

Granted- I may not completely finish it right now- but you know what? That's okay.

Because at least I'm a lot closer to finishing it then I was before I did the work, right?

The reason this works for me is that I just get bored. If I don't completely finish a project in a short period of time, I lose interest and move onto something else.

Whether it's a workout program, book, or project I'm doing for work- doesn't matter.

Eventually, I'll get tired of it.

That's why I have to work fast, and just do it now!

If it's a workout program- just go ahead and do the workout. Even if you change to a different program next week, that's fine. As long as you're doing everything you can this week to get in shape, you'll at least be better off next week than you were today, right?

Or if I'm working on my side business. Sure, maybe next week I will have something else to work on that is more exciting to me. But for now, while I'm excited about *this* project, I just need to go for it and get it done ASAP.

Have you ever heard the term "Money Loves Speed"? This is what I'm talking about.

The faster you get something out there, the faster you see if it works.

If it does, great! Keep going for it.

But if it doesn't- oh well, right? At least you know that other things will come your way.

The alternative is to just sit on it, and plan on doing it "later." But that later never comes, because new stuff will pop up instead.

So again- work fast and get it done while you're motivated to do so!

Multi-task

Don't get me wrong here- I think multitasking is very inefficient.

...if you do it the wrong way.

But there are a lot of ways to kill 2 birds with one stone, and come out on top.

The reason multitasking is inefficient is because you tend to actually get less done than if you did each thing individually.

But there are some things you can combine to make that time much more productive.

For example, these days I tend to listen to podcasts or audio books while I exercise. So I'm both learning AND getting in better shape at the same time.

Lots of people do the same thing while they're in the car.

Another good example is lunch with an old friend. Don't think of it as just lunch, but also a chance to maintain and build your business network. You never know when you might need it.

These are just a few examples, but I hope you see my point.

This is motivating to me because I have 2 things to look forward to with my workouts- learning new things *and* getting in better shape.

I'm actually a lot more excited to do it, because I know it's a great investment of my time and energy.

Just Get Started

This is similar to what I talked about earlier with working fast, but it's a bit different too.

What I've realized when it comes to getting stuff done is that besides just doing it fast, the hardest step is the first one!

For example, flossing my teeth. It's easy think that it's a pain and not worth the effort.

But if I just aim for accomplishing the first step- removing the floss from my bathroom drawer- it's a lot easier to get started.

The same goes with working out- putting your gym clothes on is the first step. Easy, right?

And once you've accomplished that first step, you have built up a little bit of momentum to do the next step.

So for working out- after putting on my gym clothes, I'm more likely to get into my car to drive to the gym. That's the second step.

And once I've done that- I'm already at the gym, I may as well exercise.

Before I know it- my workout is done, I'm showered and I'm proud of myself for going.

So you only have to be motivated for the FIRST step! Not as daunting now, is it?

CONCLUSION

Being able to motivate yourself means knowing *why* you want something to happen.

Maybe it's for health reasons.

Perhaps you want to buy your family nicer stuff.

It could be more time at home.

Whatever it is- you've GOT to set S.M.A.R.T. goals, review them regularly, stay focused on the big picture, and share your goals with the world.

For a quick pick-me-up, feel free to watch inspirational videos and quotes.

But don't rely on these things.

TRUE motivation comes only from inside, and those around you.

A video you found on YouTube can't do that.

It can help energize you for a small amount of time, but it can't sustain your motivation.

Only you can do that.

9 787096 945637

Printed by Libri Plureos GmbH in Hamburg, Germany